Hampshire

"Here's to old cricket, the grand game of cricket,
The turf and the tent, and the telegraph-boards!
A cheer for the pleasure of bat, ball, and wicket,
The pastime of peasant, the glory of lords."

W YARDLEY

Hampshire

An evocative view of Hampshire by Bob Croxford

Published by Atmosphere

To all the helpers at Atmosphere

HAMPSHIRE

Photographs copyright Bob Croxford 2001
Text copyright Bob Croxford 2001
(except where separately acknowledged).
Design copyright Ann Butcher and Atmosphere.
Anthology compilation copyright Bob Croxford.

First published by ATMOSPHERE in 2001
Willis Vean
Mullion
Helston Cornwall TR12 7DF
TEL: 01326 240 180
FAX: 01326 240 900
www.atmosphere.co.uk

ISBN 09521850 5 9

Designed by Ann Butcher
Scanning by Formatrix, Exeter & Scantec, Falmouth
Printed and bound by L.E.G.O. Italy

FRONT COVER: Wall at St. Cross Hospital
INSET: Kingsgate, Winchester
FRONTISPIECE: Broadhalfpenny Down

Also by BOB CROXFORD

FROM CORNWALL WITH LOVE	*ISBN 09521850 0 8*
FROM DEVON WITH LOVE	*ISBN 09521850 1 6*
FROM BATH WITH LOVE	*ISBN 09521850 2 4*
FROM DORSET WITH LOVE	*ISBN 09521850 3 2*
FROM THE COTSWOLDS WITH LOVE	*ISBN 09521850 4 0*
A VIEW OF AVALON (SOMERSET)	*ISBN 09521850 6 7*
THE CORNISH COAST	*ISBN 09521850 7 5*

CONTENTS

~*Introduction*~

HAMPSHIRE. The very name is redolent of so much that is ENGLAND. Sunday cricket and afternoon tea, trim cottages and trout fishing, patchwork fields and winding rivers, secluded harbours and great ports. There are so many aspects to the varied county of HAMPSHIRE it is hard to describe them all.

My first experience, as a child, was passing through on the way to SOUTHAMPTON. My family were part of the tide of emigrants escaping post-war austerity to find a better life abroad. Returning a few years later I was struck by the small scale prettiness of everything. Rows of neat houses and patchwork fields. Since then I have got to know it as a rich and varied county.

HAMPSHIRE stands square on the SOLENT, the protected estuary which became synonymous with sea travel. The English Navy was built from Hampshire oaks and sailed to defeat the Spanish, the French and the ships of many other countries. The British Empire was built by the people who sailed down the Solent and off to the New World, the West Indies, East Indies, Africa and Australia. While the north of England depended on the port of Liverpool, the travellers from the south used Southampton as their embarkation point. Writers and administrators, civil servants and soldiers all waved farewell to England from the deck of ships in the Solent. No wonder that many, when far away in foreign climes, conjured up an image of ENGLAND which was HAMPSHIRE. Air travel has taken the romance of sea voyages away but the byways and countryside of HAMPSHIRE lie largely unchanged.

Hampshire contains some large towns and cities but the countryside is always close at hand. Where else do so many unspoilt villages sit just down the road from major towns?

Much of Hampshire's history is tied to the development of the nation's power. When England was weak the Normans invaded and established WINCHESTER as their capital. The conquerors brought prosperity to the county and encouraged greater church influence. William I and his heirs created THE NEW FOREST as a hunter's playground.

The writers' quotes which accompany the pictures are from a variety of sources and periods. Some writers made their homes here and the influence of the county on their writing is unmistakable. H G Wells lived in Portsmouth, Dickens who was born there had Nicholas Nickleby arrive on foot. Arthur Conan Doyle practised as a doctor in Hampshire while writing his early historical novels.

The pictures are not intended as a direct comment on the anthology. The writing is more a counterpoint to the camera's view.

Bob Croxford 2001.

~THE BIG PORTS~

PORTSMOUTH and SOUTHAMPTON have historically been two of the most important ports in the country. While they both grew prosperous because of their unique natural harbours Portsmouth served the Royal Navy leaving Southampton to grow as a passenger port.

The significance of PORTSMOUTH was considerable in the days when the English Navy made the country a major maritime power. The Naval dockyards were at the forefront of warship design and building. The HAMPSHIRE countryside also played a part providing much of the oak timbers. Most parts of the county were also helped by the enormous amount of traffic arriving at the port. The Portsmouth Road was a famous route from London. In the days of stage coaches the route to the port was one of the most used in the country.

When HORATIO NELSON led his flagship VICTORY to fight the combined French and Spanish fleets at what would become the Battle of Trafalgar, he was leading an awesome array of warships against the strongest navy in the world. He was to fight them in their home waters where they could easily be supplied. This should have been of decisive advantage to the Spanish. H M S Victory had a full complement of 820 men crammed into her oaken hull. It was a credit to Nelson's prestige that only a handful had been press-ganged. The crew were willing because they scented victory and profitable looting and plunder of the enemy ships. Twenty two of the crew were from the United States of America, two were Canadians, Jamaica supplied one while the rest of the West Indies supplied another four. Even the land-locked Swiss provided two men.

Morale was high during the trip south to Cadiz. Nelson kept the men in a state of readiness by doing gunnery practice at sea. He had taken extra gunpowder especially. When they met the enemy his highly trained men were able to follow his original tactical manoeuvers with speed and discipline. In what was to be a memorable battle Nelson was to lose his life but win a place in the history books. Such are the associations with naval grandeur that the ship has been kept at Portsmouth as a monument to those times. It was still afloat at the beginning of the 20thC but was given greater protection in a dry dock in 1925.

SOUTHAMPTON is a natural harbour with several advantages. It is sheltered by the Isle of Wight which also creates a unique double high tide on the SOLENT. With the advent of large passenger liners SOUTHAMPTON really came into its own. Efficient boat trains from many parts of the country sped passengers to their embarkation far faster than a boat could get out of the Thames estuary. When travel to the New World became relatively commonplace every opportunity to speed the journey was important. The extra high tide meant that boats could turn around and keep a more cost effective schedule than boats operating from The Port of London.

The city supplied many of the workers on the great liners. Although they travelled far and wide the stewards, waiters, engineers and other crew had a life of very hard work with little pay. After many years at sea they often found they could not adjust to life ashore. They had little land based social life and often did not marry. Tragedy affected SOUTHAMPTON badly. The Titanic sailed from here in 1912 with many crew from the town.

During the Second World War both SOUTHAMPTON and PORTSMOUTH were targets for enemy bombers and suffered extensive damage.

*W*e drew into Portsmouth Harbour past the towering grey flanks of anchored warships and I glimpsed, swaying at its mooring further ahead, Nelson's Victory, patched and painted remnant of another war in another time. England had expected too much of her soldiers in my war and I no longer knew where my duty lay. Once the ferry had docked, I headed straight for the Mermaid. There was nowhere else to go.

ROBERT GODDARD 1988 (Fiction set in WW1)

*T*his harbour was choppy with the criss-crossed wakes of gunboats coming and going, their flags flying and their sailors scrambling over their decks. I identified this activity with the Falklands news and I assumed these boats were setting out that day for the South Atlantic. Portsmouth harbour contained a flotilla of Royal Navy ships, giving solemn hoots on their horns. Looking north towards the Royal Dockyard I could see the topmost sections of the masts of H.M.S. Victory, but it was the gunboats in the harbour that were bucking the waves. These days, many harbours I saw looked self-important and purposeful and over-cautious: they were battle-ready. The Falklands war depended almost entirely on the strength of the British fleet and it had brought the cold excitement of patriotism to these harbours.

PAUL THEROUX 1983

◀ *H M S Victory*
Ship's Figurehead ▶

*T*he Situation of this Place is ſuch, that it is choſen, as may well be ſaid, for the beſt Security to the Navy above all the Places in Britain; the Entrance into the Harbour is ſafe, but very narrow, guarded on both ſides by terrible Platforms of Cannon, particularly on the Point; which is a Suburb of Portſmouth properly ſo call'd, where there is a Brick Platform built with Two Tire of Guns, One over another, and which can Fire ſo in Cover, that the Gunners cannot be beaten from their Guns, or their Guns eaſily diſmounted; the other is from the Point of Land on the ſide of Goſport, which they call Gilkicker, where alſo they have Two Batteries.

DANIEL DEFOE   1727

*T*hen the green height of Portsdown Hill tempted them, and leaving their machines in the village, they clambered up the slope to the silent red-brick fort that crowned it. Thence they had a view of Portsmouth and its cluster of sister towns, the crowded narrows of the harbour, the Solent, and the Isle of Wight like a blue cloud through the hot haze. Jessie by some miracle had become a skirted woman in the Cosham inn. Mr Hoopdriver lounged gracefully on the turf, smoked a Red Herring cigarette, and lazily regarded the fortified town that spread like a map away there, the inner line of defence like toy fortifications, a mile off perhaps; and beyond that a few little fields and then the beginnings of Landport suburb and the smoky cluster of the multitudinous houses.

H G WELLS   1896

There is no lack of comfortable furnished apartments in
Portsmouth, and no difficulty in finding some that are
proportionate to very slender finances; but the former were too good,
and the latter too bad, and they went into so many houses, and came
out unsuited, that Nicholas seriously began to think he should be
obliged to ask permission to spend the night in the theatre, after all.

Eventually, however, they stumbled upon two small rooms up three
pair of stairs, or rather two pair and a ladder, at a tobacconist's shop,
on the Common Hard: a dirty street leading down to the dockyard.
These Nicholas engaged, only too happy to have escaped any request
for payment of a week's rent beforehand.

CHARLES DICKENS   1838-39 *(Nicholas Nickleby)*

The Government of the Place is by a Mayor and Aldermen, &c. as in other Corporations, and the Civil Government is no more interrupted by the Military, than if there was no Garriſon there, ſuch is the good Conduct of the Governors, and ſuch it has always been, ſince our Soveraigns have ceas'd to encourage the Soldiery to Inſult the Civil Magiſtrates: And we have very ſeldom had any Complaint on either ſide, either of want of Diſcipline among the Soldiers, or want of Prudence in the Magiſtrates: The Inhabitants indeed neceſſarily ſubmit to ſuch Things as are the Conſequence of a Garriſon Town, ſuch as being Examin'd at the Gates, ſuch as being obliged to keep Garriſon Hours, and not be let out, or let in after Nine a Clock at Night, and the like; but theſe are Things no People will count a Burthen, where they get their Bread by the very Situation of the Place, as is the caſe here.

DANIEL DEFOE   1727

◀ *South Parade Pier, Southsea*
Southsea Castle ▶

*F*rom *this school we were led against the enemy, a body of French, three thousand two hundred strong, who had occupied Portchester Castle, near Portsmouth. It must not indeed be dissembled that our enemies were naked unarmed prisoners, the object of pity rather than of terror; their misery was somewhat alleviated by public and private bounty; but their sufferings exhibited the evils of war, and their noisy spirits the character of the nation.*

EDWARD GIBBON   1793

◀ *Portchester Castle*
Titchfield Castle ▶

More travellers to and from England use Southampton than use any other English port; it is her principal gateway for her colonial subjects, the principal destination or point of call for trans-Atlantic ships, and several services ply between French Channel ports and Southampton.

How many of all these scores of thousands who pass through Southampton each year do so otherwise than by boat-trains to and from the docks, I have no means of knowing. But I am sure that a very great number of those who think of Southampton only as a transfer-place would be delighted, and richly rewarded, if they would make it a place of sojourn for several days after debarking or before sailing.

CLARA E LAUGHLIN   1926

It would be impossible to say where Southampton itself really began, though I should like to believe that the true boundary is that corner of East Park where there is a memorial to the lost engineers of the Titanic, to prove that there are dangerous trades here too. Further down, the London Road changes into Above Bar Street; then the traffic swirls about the Bar Gate itself, which is very old but has so many newly-painted armorial decorations that it looks as gaudy as the proscenium of a toy theatre; and then once through or round Bar Gate, you are in High Street. Another quarter of a mile or so, at the bottom of High Street, you must go carefully; otherwise you may lose England altogether and find yourself looking at the Woolworth building or table mountain. One could write a story of a man who walked down this long straight street, on a dark winter's day, and kept on and on until at last he saw that he had walked into a panelled smoke room, where he settled down for a pipe, only to discover soon that Southampton had quietly moved away from him and that his smoke room was plunging about in the Channel. For, you see, you can catch the Berengaria or the Empress of Britain at the end of this High Street.

J B PRIESTLEY   1933

*F*ROME THENS *we went to Tichfield, th'erle of Southampton's house, and so on to Southampton toune. The citisens had bestowed for our comeng great cost in peinting, repairing and ramparing of their wallis. The toune is ansome, and for the bignes of it as faire houses as be at London. The citeseins made great chere, and many of them kept costly tables.*

EDWARD VI   1552

*W*hoosh

Two bombs fell nearby, it could have been us. We heard a whoosh and it was just like the air being sucked out of your body. We were in this cupboard, under the stairs. My husband had said, 'we won't go to the shelter tonight.' This was just as well because it got mucked about by the blast. I had some washing on the line; it was covered in dust. We were evacuated to Frome after that. I said if I ever go back, I'm not hanging the washing out!

EMILY LOADER

1940s Reminiscence

◀ *Merchant's House, Southampton*
Bar Gate, Southampton ▶

~Villages~

Although HAMPSHIRE has many large towns its character is determined by its many picturesque villages. The county is a fertile, well watered agricultural area. Its farmers grew rich with the convenient trade from country markets to the big cities of Portsmouth and Southampton and also used the good communications with London to have a good trade with the capital.

Life in Hampshire's villages was often based on serving the agricultural economy. It was in the villages that the smith had his forge, saddle and harness makers worked, shoe and boot makers had their workshops, carters and carriers operated. What William Cobbett called the "cottage economy" was a semi self-sufficient lifestyle. Cottage gardens would be big enough to grow a plentiful supply of vegetables, keep a pig or two, rear chickens, ducks, geese, guinea fowl and perhaps rabbit. The cottager would work at his skill in a small workshop, perhaps making farmer's boots and leather aprons, wooden forks and arrish rakes, horse shoes and other iron work, furniture, carts and spare cartwheels. All the myriad items needed by country folk would then be taken to the local market.

The annual harvest fairs were the largest. First the farmer would sell his produce and then he would visit the tradesmen. Directing the delivery of his purchases to his farm wagon, the farmer would then repair to a nearby hostelry, sit down to a mug of ale, a bag of money and settle with his suppliers. Cobbett wrote at a time when paper money first appeared, something which he railed against. Although the artisans and other suppliers would be paid promptly they had the difficult task of financing the work itself. Many items were only in demand at certain seasons while the craftsman had to work all year building up a stock.

Hampshire's villages owe their character to the wonderfully varied vernacular building styles. Cottages are constructed by whatever materials are at hand. Timber framed houses with either brick or wood and plaster infills, characteristic flint and brick, shiplap boards and brick construction can be seen side by side. Choice of materials depended on price and skills available rather than aesthetic merit. It is only in a more modern age that we see the beauty in many of these old and simple buildings.

WHEREWELL makes a good job of hiding the River Test by presenting some beguiling old cottages to face the road and the rushing cars. Apart from some very attractive thatched cottages the village has a few half hidden openings to the river.

EAST MEON sits astride the River Meon where Isaak Walton wrote in praise of the leisurely pastime of angling.

KINGSCLERE is a typical North Downs village with a church dating from Norman times.

Would anyone find their way off the main road to the otherwise sleepy village of CHAWTON were it not for the signs announcing JANE AUSTEN'S HOUSE? It was here that the famous novelist lived from 1809 to 1817 with her mother and sister. She often walked in the surrounding countryside indulging in the relatively new fashion for admiring the picturesque beauty of the countryside.

Almost hiding behind Portsdown the tiny village of SOUTHWICK has some of the most characterful cottages in the whole County. However in a place like Hampshire it faces stiff competition in the prettiness stakes.

LONGPARISH could easily claim the title of the thatched cottage capital of England. Stretching along the RIVER TEST it has a few bridges where short glimpses of water can be seen.

HURSLEY has many historic associations especially when Oliver Cromwell's son, Richard married a local girl in 1643. Unsuccessful as Lord Protector of the Commonwealth Richard retired to Hursley in 1659. He and his wife fled to France when Charles II restored the monarchy.

SELBORNE will be forever associated with REV. GILBERT WHITE the 18thC naturalist who wrote The Natural History of Selborne. One can still walk the paths he described 250 years ago including the famous zig-zag up the Hangar behind his house. In the village one can visit his house which is now the Gilbert White's House & The Oates Museum.

*T*his, to my fancy, is a very nice country. It is continual hill and dell. Now and then a chain of hills higher than the rest, and these are downs or woods. To stand upon any of the hills and look around you, you almost think you see the ups and downs of the sea in a heavy swell (as the sailors call it) after what they call a gale of wind. The undulations are endless, and the great variety in the height, breadth, length, and form of the little hills, has a very delightful effect. - The soil, which, to look on it, appears to be more than half flint stones, is very good in quality, and, in general, better on the tops of the lesser hills than in the valleys. It has great tenacity; does not wash away like sand, or light loam. It is a stiff, tenacious loam, mixed with flint stones. Bears saint-foin well, and all sorts of grass, which makes the fields on the hills as green as meadows, even at this season; and the grass does not burn up in summer.

WILLIAM COBBETT   Nov 4th 1821

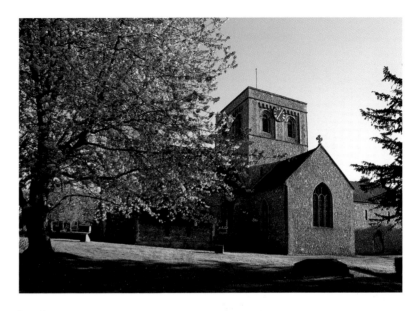

*T*he more we think of Hampshire and the more we look at its map or ride about its million acres, the more we feel that this central mass of southern England is something unique. Nature has richly equipped it with its share of common English beauty, and History, as we see, has adorned it beyond most other shires.

ARTHUR MEE   1939

My dearest Cassandra

Fanny takes my mother to Alton this morning, which gives me an opportunity of sending you a few lines without any other trouble than that of writing them.

This is a delightful day in the country, and I hope not much too hot for town. Well, you had a good journey, I trust, and all that, and not rain enough to spoil your bonnet. It appeared so likely to be a wet evening that I went up to the Gt. House between three and four, and dawdled away an hour very comfortably, though Edwd. was not very brisk. The air was clearer in the evening and he was better. We all five walked together into the kitchen garden and along the Gosport road, and they drank tea with us.

Yours very affectionately,   J. Austen

Tuesday 13th June 1814,

O ur Chawton home, how much we find
    Already in it, to our mind;

And how convinced that when complete

It will all other houses beat

That ever have been made or mended,

With rooms concise, or rooms distended...

JANE AUSTEN 1809

◀ Jane Austen's House, Chawton
Thatched cottage ▶

*I*t has occurred to me that real people still live in the English countryside~live on it~and they are not exhibits for inspections by "foreigners". Their existence is often not simple and lovely. They are inclined to be earthy. They are dying out, and no amount of preservation of Rural England will keep them alive unless they are considered as the human beings who made that England, and who alone can keep it fit to be even a garden suburb. Motorists, hikers, week-enders~these also, doubtless, are God's creatures and have a place in the scheme of things; but they would have no country sights to see if it were not for the people they patronise in the villages. England, in its rural areas, is once more in danger of becoming two nations.

F J HARVEY DARTON   1927

I have just returned from Southampton. Have you ever been at that lovely spot, which combines all that is enchanting in wood and land and water with all that is "buxom, blythe, and debonair" in society ~ that charming town, which is not a watering place only because it is something better? Do not be afraid of a long description. The scenery of the south of Hampshire is of all others the most difficult to describe; for it is not the picturesque which may be thrown off in a few careless strokes; or the sublime which, with the wish to delineate it, almost inspires the power; but the beautiful ~ sometimes in its gayest, and sometimes in its softest dress ~ but always the beautiful, of which the prevailing and pervading charm is not the woods or streams or villages, nor even the sparkling ocean, but the exquisite arrangement and combination of the whole. Southampton has, however, in my eyes an attraction independent even of its scenery, in the total absence of the vulgar hurry of business or the chilling apathy of fashion.

MARY MITFORD 1812

◄ *Cottage in Southwick*
Hursley ►

It is a pleasure to be at Selborne; nevertheless I find I always like Selborne best when I am out of it, especially when I am rambling about that bit of beautiful country on the border of which it lies. The memory of Gilbert White; the old church with its low, square tower and its famous yew tree; above all, the constant sight of the Hanger clothed in its beechen woods ~ green, or bronze and red-gold, or purple-brown in leafless winter ~ all these things do not prevent a sense of lassitude, of ill-being, which I experience in the village when I am too long in it, and which vanishes when I quit it, and seem to breathe a better air.

W H HUDSON   1923

The manor of Selborne, was it strictly looked after, with all it's kindly aspects, and all it's sloping coverts, would swarm with game; even now hares, partridges, and pheasants abound; and in old days woodcocks were as plentiful. There are few quails, because they more affect open fields than enclosures; after harvest some few land-rails are seen.

The parish of Selborne, by taking in so much of the forest, is a vast district. Those who tread the bounds are employed part of three days in the business, and are of opinion that the outline, in all it's curves and indentings, does not comprise less than thirty miles.

The village stands in a sheltered spot, secured by The Hanger from the strong westerly winds. The air is soft, but rather moist from the effluvia of so many trees; yet perfectly healthy and free from agues. The quantity of rain that falls on it is very considerable, as may be supposed in so woody and mountainous a district.

GILBERT WHITE   1789

~Small Towns~

The prosperity of Hampshire has led to the development of some fine towns. Many grew up around a bridge or other river crossing point. A bridge was a convenient place to hold a market and a convenient place for an inn, stables and other facilities. Frequently the significance of a church and its benefactors would lead to the growth of a village into a town.

In this book I've mixed some towns with villages. Some towns have a laid back village feel while some villages bustle as busily as a town. I apologise now if anyone is offended by my choices. There is so much in a book of this size which has to be left out.

The Abbey at ROMSEY was founded in the 10thC and rose in importance while Winchester was the capital of Norman England. The bulky church was enlarged by the Normans in the 12thC. The Abbey became one of the largest in southern England. Henry VIII sold it for £100 at the Dissolution of the Monasteries. Lord Palmerston lived just across the river at Broadlands and is remembered by a statue dominating the main square.

PETERSFIELD is a typical Hampshire market town with a distinctive planned look with wide streets and elegant houses. Many of the eastern towns owe a lot of their historic importance to their proximity to the Portsmouth Road. Staging Inns flourished as well as the attendant need to horses, waggoners, coaches and victuals.

If any town in Hampshire has "gone commercial" it is ANDOVER. Ringed by innumerable ring roads it is hard to find the centre. That it has a noble history is proved by the signs above the various Inns and Pubs. The amount of Royalty who have stayed at the town throughout the centuries prove that the town was an important crossroads.

BISHOP'S WALTHAM is visited because of the ruined palace dating from the 12thC. The town has a charming ambiance with narrow lanes, characterful houses and useful old-fashioned shops.

FORDINGBRIDGE is just what it says in the name. A bridge here crosses the HAMPSHIRE AVON and has done since replacing an ancient ford. The seven arched Great Bridge dates from 1286 but may be even older.

STOCKBRIDGE was once an important stop on the great road west but traffic has now found other routes and left the large village relatively quiet. With the River Test just at the end of the road this is definitely fishing country. Some anglers down from London know no other place in Hampshire but Stockbridge and a few hundred metres of fishing. Fishing which reputedly costs more than anywhere else in England.

ALTON is another of those towns on Hampshire's eastern edge which thrived on the transport through the town. Naturally beer was brewed to quench the traveller's thirst. Brewing later became a speciality in the town. Early writers are a bit snooty about the town's weaving potential.

NEW ALRESFORD is classed as a village but I've elevated it to a town because it has one attribute that even lots of towns do not possess. A railway station. And not just any old trains but real working steam trains which will take you through scenic splendour all the way to Alton where you can connect with the main line. THE WATERCRESS LINE as it is called was axed nearly fifty years ago and has been saved by volunteer enthusiasts who preserve a collection of steam trains, vintage carriages and period stations.

Alresford is NEW ALRESFORD on the maps and signposts but referred to as "Awlsford" by locals. Here the plan is typical of many Hampshire towns and villages which follow a T layout. The town is on a main road, in this case the Winchester to London road, with buildings either side. Then another road enters from one side which serves the local industry or trade. In Alresford the speciality is watercress which grows on cultivated beds sluiced by the RIVER ITCHEN. In many cases this transverse street is wide enough for a market.

If despite the traffic you notice a certain harmony in the town it is because the town was almost totally destroyed by fire in 1689. Fires also occurred in the following century making New Alresford a relatively rebuilt town.

*R*omsey, in the magic county of Hampshire, is the ideal small market town. Lord Palmerston, with bronze hair turned green by years of rain, stands importantly on a plinth in the market-place; a policeman in an easier attitude stands near him; there is a full cake-shop opposite; everything is slowed down to a reasonable pace; men in leggings stand on the kerbstone with the expressions of deep thinkers; now and then a man and a cow cross the square.

HV MORTON   1927

The old market town of Petersfield is one of those quiet places which, to the casual stranger, seem to sleep for six days of the week, and for one day of every seven wake up to quite a sprightly and business like mood. But Petersfield is even quieter than that. Its market is but fortnightly, and for thirteen days out of every fourteen the town dozes tranquilly. The imagination pictures the inhabitants of this old municipal and parliamentary borough rubbing their eyes and yawning every alternative Wednesday, when the corn and cattle market is held; and when the last drover has gone, at the close of day, sinking again into slumber with a sigh of relief.

CHARLES G HARPER   1895

*B*ut taken as a whole Hampshire is beyond any measure of doubt the most English of English counties. And that is a better title than any conferred by good looks.

BRIAN VESEY-FITZGERALD   1940

*O*ur charabanc driver at this point required us to return in order that the tourists should be home to lunch, so we reluctantly had to let them go and solace ourselves with the sight of God's Hill and Fordingbridge and the valley of Avon to Ringwood.
S P B MAIS   1927

*A*lton and Farnham Machine sets out every Monday, Wednesday, and Friday morning, at 6 o'clock from the White Hart in Alton to the Goat's Head Inn, Farnham, and from thence to the New Inn in the Old Bailey, Ludgate Hill, London, and returns every Tuesday, Thursday, and Saturday, at 8 o'clock in the morning, to the Goat's Head Inn in Farnham, and the White Hart in Alton.

Each passenger to pay to and from Alton 10s., and Farnham, 8s. Fourteen pounds of Luggage allowed, all over to pay a Halfpenny a Pound.

Children on the Lap and Outside passengers to pay Half Price. Three places for Alton, and Three for Farnham.

N.B.- No Plate, Jewels, Writing, or other things of value will be accounted for, except entered as such, and paid for accordingly.

Performed, if God permit, by E. Gilbert, A. Rowley and Co

*R*ailways have killed road travel, and the present generation little knows its loss. England - rural England, that is - away from busy towns, railways, and tourist-haunted regions, where big hotels abound, and where enterprise has done its best to mar its original unaffected beauty, is indeed a very pleasant land, one surely as well worth exploring as the everlasting Continent.

JAMES JOHN HISSEY   1886

A lresford was a flouriſhing Market Town, and remarkable for this; That tho' it had no great Trade, and particularly very little, if any Manufactures, yet there was no Collection in the Town for the Poor, nor any Poor low enough to take Alms of the Pariſh, which is what I do not think can be ſaid of any Town in England beſides.

But this happy Circumſtance, which ſo diſtinguiſh'd Alresford from all her Neighbours, was brought to an End in the Year----, when, by a ſudden and ſurprizing Fire, the whole Town, with both the Church and the Market-Houſe, was reduc'd to a heap of Rubbiſh; and, except a few poor Hutts at the remoteſt Ends of the Town, not a Houſe left ſtanding:...

DANIEL DEFOE   1727

The Romans established a base on the RIVER ITCHEN which must have been one of their best locations in Britain. What they called *Vent-Castra* became the Saxon capital of WINCHESTER. Today one senses that perhaps Winchester feels a bit let down. The former capital of England and the Wessex Kingdom has now become famous for traffic jams and by-passes. However, on foot, WINCHESTER is a delight.

Coming from one direction a statue of King Alfred the Great greets you. Few sculptures epitomise the rugged romance of early England so well. A short walk up Broadway is the new Victorian Guildhall. Built on a bold romantic gothic style it shows that the city's good burghers were not lacking in confidence 150 years ago. Walking up the High Street one could easily become distracted and miss a small alleyway to the left. With coy modesty it seems that WINCHESTER is trying to hide its prize possession. Here is Europe's second longest Cathedral, second only to St Peter's in Rome.

It was built in a number of styles after the Normans made this their capital in 1066. Enthusiasm for the monumental style proved the undoing of the Norman structure. A spire collapsed in 1107 which has never been rebuilt. A century later the building was extended to the east using logs and wooden beams as foundations on the marshy ground. As these rotted away the whole building began to sink and tilt. Nearly a hundred years ago a diver, WILLIAM WALKER, spent almost every day for five years replacing the wooden beams with bags of cement.

This grand building was the church of the powerful for many years. Kings and princes married their queens and princesses here.

The establishment of WINCHESTER school improved the City's reputation far and wide.

Beautifully situated across from the water meadows is the HOSPITAL OF ST. CROSS. This range of buildings is essentially a set of almshouses but also has a function serving sustenance to any traveller who asks for it. Although this is now considered a quaint custom there have been many even in the 20thC who appreciated this act of simple charity.

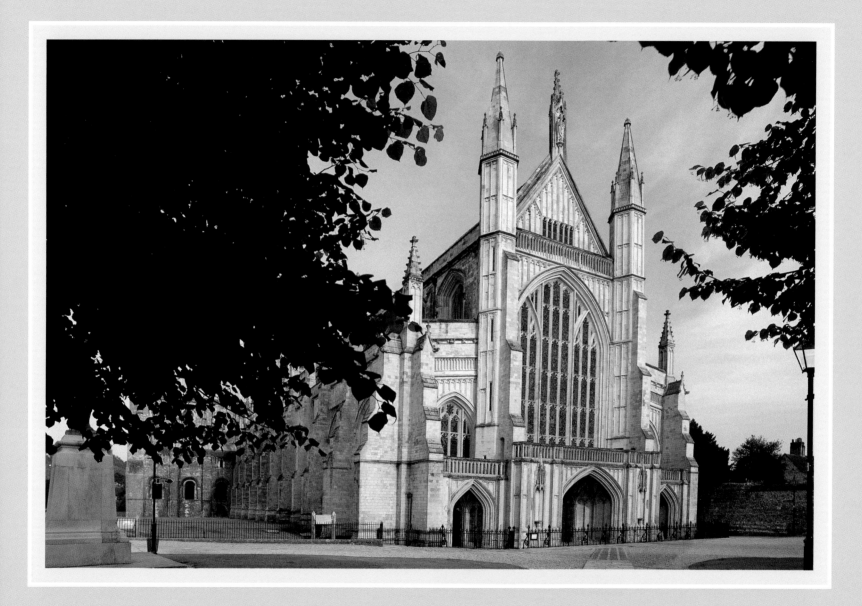

Thus it was that Winchester grew to be the most important place in south England. How early we do not know, but certainly deeper than even tradition or popular song can go it gathered round itself the first functions of leadership. It was possessed of a sanctity which it has not wholly lost. It preserves, from its very decay, a full suggestion of its limitless age. Its trees, its plan, and the accent of the spoken language in its streets are old. It maintains the irregularities and accretions in building which are, as it were, the outer shell of antiquity in a city.

HILAIRE BELLOC   1904

◀ *King Alfred's Statue*
Winchester ▶

*O*nce when he went as a judge on the Western Circuit, he was invited with several members of the Bar to dine with the Dean of Winchester, whom he had never met before. A few days afterwards a friend asked the Dean what he thought of Baron Martin.

'Well,' was the reply, 'he does not appear to me to be a man of enlarged information. He actually never had heard of William of Wykeham, and wanted to know who he was.'

Baron Martin was asked by some one what he thought of the Dean of Winchester.

'Well,' said he, 'I can't say I think much of him. He seems very deficient in a knowledge of what is going on in the world; he absolutely did not know what horse had won the last Derby.'

ANON

*J*ust before entering Winchester we stopped at the Church of Saint
Cross, and after looking through the quaint antiquity, we
demanded a piece of bread and draught of beer, which the founder,
Henry de Blois, in 1136, commanded should be given to every one who
should ask it at the gate. We had both, from the old couple who take
care of the church. Some twenty people every day, they said, make the
same demand. This hospitality of seven hundred years' standing did
not hinder Carlyle from pronouncing a malediction on the priest who
receives £2,000 a year, that were meant for the poor, and spends a
pittance on this small-beer and crumbs.

RALPH WALDO EMERSON   1898

◀ *Winchester Cathedral*

St Cross Hospital ▶

~THE DOWNS~

There can be few cultivated landscapes as pleasing as the SOUTH DOWNS of England. In HAMPSHIRE the steep slopes of the chalk hills are what many think of as perfect scenery.

Millions of years ago in the CRETACEOUS PERIOD what is now southern England was covered by sea. Countless numbers of shelled creatures lived and died in this sea. The detritus of their bodies built up layers on the sea bed. This became chalk. Sea currents brought a sandy mixture onto these layers which formed hard flint nodules. Millions of years passed while this layer became thicker and thicker. In the TERTIARY PERIOD of tectonic movement the land was pushed upwards. Although not as dramatic as the upheavals that formed the Alps the movement was sufficient to lift the chalk, flint and overlying layer above sea level. Erosion caused the chalk and flint strata to be exposed in the SOUTH DOWNS. At the same time the northern face

tilted downwards into what became the Thames Valley.

Chalk acts as a filter for rain water percolating through the surface. THE DOWNS act like a huge sponge allowing most surface water to run off fairly rapidly while the artesian layers are replenished over a period of years. So efficient is the chalk as a filter that there was even a proposal in the 1960s to pump sea water up to the top of the downs and allow it to replenish the water supply in the Thames Basin. The salt would have been filtered out by the chalk.

What has made the landscape we know today is the hand of man over several millennia. Early inhabitants were hunter gatherers but gathered firewood for cooking and warmth. There have been suggestions that they cleared the hilltops first as a defensive strategy. However, there are alternative ideas which suggest that war, attacks and the need for defence only occured when arable

farming had developed along with the ability to store valuable food in the form of dry grain. Whatever theory one follows the upland downs were being cleared by human intervention.

The flint layers were exploited for tool heads and used for arrows, axes, saws and knives. Five thousand years ago flint tools were exported to Europe.

WILLIAM COBBETT was familiar with these downs during his many Rural Rides as he describes here:
Uphusband, once more, and, for the sixth time this year, over the North Hampshire Hills, which, not withstanding their everlasting flints, I like very much. As you ride along even in a green lane the horses' feet make a noise like hammering. It seems as you were riding on a mass of iron. Yet the soil is good, and bears some of the best wheat in England. All these high, and indeed, all chalky lands, are excellent for sheep. But, on the top of some of these hills, there are as fine meadows as I ever saw.

*I*t was the evening of the following day. The north-facing
escarpment of Watership Down, in shadow since early morning, now
caught the western sun for an hour before twilight. Three hundred feet
the down rose vertically in a stretch of no more than six hundred ~ a
precipitous wall, from the thin belt of trees at the foot to the ridge
where the steep flattened out. The light, full and smooth, lay like a
gold rind over the turf, the furze and yew bushes, the few wind-stunted
thorn trees. From the ridge, the light seemed to cover all the slope
below, drowsy and still.

RICHARD ADAMS   1972

*B*ut this policy of uniformity, brutal as it is, is not confined to the vegetable kingdom. The once genial and exclusive Gypsies, forest-dwellers since before Shakespeare's time, are now being chivvied with their beasts into the pestilential quagmires of the lately established Concentration Camps, where under pain of crippling fines, they languish in forced association with shiftless hedge-crawlers from the towns in whose company they would not normally be seen dead. Such conditions are not favourable to anyone and least of all to Gypsies, who with the loss of their freedom and with it their ancient language and traditions soon decline in health and morale. Who then does benefit?

AUGUSTUS JOHN   1958

*H*alf-way up I found the cyclists ~ two young ladies ~ resting on the turf by the side of the Zigzag. They were conversing together as I went by, and one having asked some question which I did not hear, the other replied, "Oh no! he lived a very long time ago, and wrote a history of Selborne. About birds and that." To which the other returned, "Oh!" and then they talked of something else.

W H HUDSON   1923

◀ Romany Church near Bramdean

A walk near Selborne ▶

~THE COAST~

HAMPSHIRE has been built by and depended on the sea. PORTSMOUTH and SOUTHAMPTON attest to that. Strangely the coastline has none of the drama or beauty of other counties. Where the land ends the object is to look out to sea. To watch departing and arriving boats. The sea is to be used for war or trade and increasingly for pleasure. The sea has been a means of getting to and from foreign ports. It is a business, a vehicle of trade and supplier of work and prosperity. It is somewhere for going and coming, purposeful activity and earnest endeavour. More recently it has become a playground. Everything from surfboards to ocean going yachts, jet-skis to cruise liners can be seen from HAMPSHIRE'S shores.

There are almost no sandy beaches except at the lowest of tides. Clean washed shingle give Hampshire's foreshore a distinctive South Coast sound. The greatest volume is when thousands of tiny pebbles appear to race back into the sea with each receding wave.

Walking down the main street of EMSWORTH is like entering a funnel as the street gets narrower and narrower. Only those with the ability to turn on a proverbial sixpence should attempt to drive. At the end is a small harbour devoted to small craft. Sailing dinghies and paddle boats abound. The shelter of CHICHESTER HARBOUR make it safe for novice sailors and small children are often seen skillfully handling small boats.

LANGSTONE is a small village wedged between the sea and the sprawl of Havant to the north. A distinctive black domesticated windmill reflects in the calm waters of Chichester Harbour. The Romans built a causewayed bridge here. Remains of earlier bridges lie in the shallows beside the existing bridge.

A feature of the HAMPSHIRE coast is an almost straight edge facing the sea which is eroded by river and tide into numerous harbours. HAYLING fills a gap between CHICHESTER and LANGSTONE harbours which are almost lagoons. Hayling is flat and featureless with a beach on the sides facing the open sea. In winter it is quiet and almost empty but on sunny days in summer the beaches come to startling life. All kinds of water sports entertain those relaxing on the beaches.

HAMBLE and the HAMBLE RIVER are a yachting mecca. Everywhere is a sea of masts.

FAREHAM is not really a coastal harbour but the small area of quays give the waterfront a nautical feel.

LEE-ON-SOLENT has a laid back feel compared to the rush and bustle of PORTSMOUTH and GOSPORT. This is a place to eat an ice-cream on the Promenade, sit in a cafe and take things easy. HILL HEAD next door has bathing huts on the beach.

Of all the places along HAMPSHIRE'S coast LYMINGTON has seen the changes in boating the most. Recently it was a fairly quiet fishing quay that interested visitors. Now it has exploited the yachting mania and caters for the weekend sailor rather than the seafarer.

A happy countrey in the foure elements, if culinary fire in
courtesie may pass for one, with plenty of the best wood for the
fuel thereof; most pure and piercing the aire of this shyre; and none
in England hath more plenty of clear and fresh rivulets of troutful
water, not to speak of the friendly sea, conveniently distanced from
London. As foe the earth, " he continues, "it is both fair and fruitful,
and may pass for an expedient betwixt pleasure and profit, where by
mutual consent they are moderately accommodated."

FULLER

H ampshire is essentially an attractive county
antiquity, historic association, harmony of form,
and a rich glow of colour,- all these and more Hampshire
has to offer, and in these there are few spots in England
to rival her. As the Home-shire, or cradle of Saxon rule in
our land, Hampshire will always occupy a leading
position among English counties.

REV. TELFORD VARLEY 1909

◄ *Langstone*
Hayling Island ►

*T*he village of Hamble lies upon the Hamble River, a tidal tributary of Southampton Water, about six miles as the crow flies from Southampton. In the last century Hamble was a fishing village; by 1914 it had become a prosperous centre for the building, fitting out, and laying up of yachts. In later years an aerodrome, a seaplane station, and three small aircraft factories came into being near the village, while the yachting industry increased enormously. In consequence the village spread out in a rash of villas, clubs, and week-end cottages.

NEVIL SHUTE   1939

*W*e had passed through Fareham and Botley during this conversation, and were now making our way down the Bishopstoke road. The soil changes about here from chalk to sand, so that our horses' hoofs did but make a dull subdued rattle, which was no bar to our talk - or rather to my companion's, for I did little more than listen. In truth, my mind was so full of anticipations of what was before us, and of thoughts of the home behind, that I was in no humour for sprightly chatter. The sky was somewhat clouded, but the moon glinted out between the rifts, showing us the long road which wound away in front of us. On either side were scattered houses with gardens sloping down toward the road. The heavy, sickly scent of strawberries was in the air.

SIR ARTHUR CONAN DOYLE   1887

*S*ailors earned their money like horses and spent it like asses.

ANON

After a charming ride through long avenues of noble oaks, the materials of future navies, they came again into a flat, open country, and soon after arrived at Lymington, a small place, but commodious and inviting, by its pleasant walks and rides, to those who resort to the sea for the purpose of bathing.

PRISCILLA WAKEFIELD   1806

The snow lay several feet high round the cottage, being driven against it by the wind. They had kept a passage clear to the yard, and had kept the yard as clear of snow as possible; they could do no more. A sharp frost and clear weather succeeded to the snowstorms, and there appeared no chance of the snow melting away. The nights were dark and long, and their oil for their lamp was getting low. Humphrey was anxious to go to Lymington, as they required many things; but it was impossible to go anywhere except on foot, and walking was, from the depth of the snow, a most fatiguing exercise. There was one thing, however, that Humphrey had not forgotten, which was, that he had told Edward that he would try and capture some of the forest ponies; and during the whole of the time since the heavy fall of snow had taken place he had been making his arrangements.

CAPTAIN MARRYAT   1847

The Children of the New Forest

~THE RIVERS~

Dripping and gurgling, sparkling and bubbling, gliding and racing water flows everywhere. The rivers of HAMPSHIRE are famous for their beauty, their tranquillity and above all for their fishing. The chalk downs act like giant sponges soaking up rainwater and releasing it at a steady rate. Even in high summer the clear waters flow swift through willow tree shade. There is something almost sacred about HAMPSHIRE rivers. Unlike other counties there seems to have been little attempt at commercial navigation. They are left to discover on quiet walks.

Although much of the river bank is a private domain we shouldn't begrudge the riparian landlords their protective attitude. HAMPSHIRE rivers are like jewels, valuable and jealously guarded. In many places the rivers are open for walking. Trout can be seen in the clear waters while a sudden flash of bright blue could be a kingfisher.

The lime rich water of HAMPSHIRE'S rivers seems to have an especially clear quality. I have seen the bottom stirred up by horses hooves as they wade through a ford and the cloudiness drop back to the bottom within seconds.

The RIVER AVON has been a moveable boundary between HAMPSHIRE and DORSET. If we have another local government re-organisation it will no doubt be used again. Rising outside the county the river makes a useful edge to the NEW FOREST.

Of all HAMPSHIRE'S rivers the RIVER TEST is probably the most famous. Like several of Hampshire's streams it rises below the chalk downs of the interior and travels west before finding a way through the hills and turning south. Passing through OVERTON, WHITCHURCH and LONGPARISH it is joined by many small streams along its way. The ANTON RIVER appears to

come from nowhere and exist fully fledged at ANDOVER just a short distance from its source. South of ANDOVER the ANTON joins the TEST and makes it a serious river. Sometimes racing in wide shallow sweeps and at other times slow as the bed gets deeper. Sometimes loitering in the shade of a clump of willows and sometimes idling in the sun across a water meadow.

STOCKBRIDGE is skirted and then the river divides several times on its way to ROMSEY. After Romsey the river is still in the country until suddenly, almost without warning the TEST has reached SOUTHAMPTON. The estuary here is called the RIVER TEST but surely this is a bit tongue in cheek. Do we really expect those huge ocean liners to float on the water from a modest trout stream?

If the TEST is HAMPSHIRE'S premier fishing river the ITCHEN runs it a close second. The RIVER

ITCHEN rises just east of NEW ALRESFORD. The water is pure and clean and perfect for growing the watercress that Alresford is famous for. WINCHESTER is the next notable visitor for this fast flowing river. Various mills have existed along the river from early times. Heading south the ITCHEN also ends up in SOUTHAMPTON water.

*W*hen I think of Hampshire, it is
seldom of the forest that I think, but
more of the multitudinous ribbons of shining
clear blue water in her chalk streams,
cutting up the meads into a thousand queer
shapes, fringed with slender swaying poplars
and stockish pollarded willows. What a riot
of buttercups and marsh-marigolds these Test
and Avon and Itchen valleys are.

S P B MAIS 1927

*W*e will wander ~ for though the sun be bright, here are good
fish to be picked out of sharps and stopholes ~ into the
water-tables, ridged up centuries since into furrows forty feet broad
and five feet high, over which the crystal water sparkles among the
roots of the rich grass, and hurries down innumerable drains to find
its parent stream between tufts of great blue geranium, and spires of
purple loosestrife, and the delicate white and pink comfrey-bells, and
the avens fairest and most modest of all the water-side nymphs, who
hangs her head all day long in pretty shame, with a soft blush upon
her tawny cheek. But at the mouth of each of those drains, if we can
get our flies in, and keep ourselves unseen, we will have one cast at
least. For at each of them, in some sharp-rippling spot, lies a great
trout or two, waiting for beetle, caterpillar, and whatsoever else may
be washed from among the long grass above.

CHARLES KINGSLEY 1889

*T*he river still runs as smoothly as ever it did. The springs from the chalk feed it all the way - clear and pure. The watercress grows wild in it - but much is cultivated and sent up to London. So pure is the water that I have bathed in it ever since I was a boy. I still do. I swim in it ~ swallowing mouthfuls ~ and never come to any harm. I have leaned over the bank and 'tickled' the trout in it when I was very young. I do not fish it now. I like to see the trout lying just below the surface ~ to watch the river for the fly ~ sometimes to see the fish jump right out. There is always something to see by our river. The kingfisher darting bright blue - the heron standing dead still waiting to strike - the coots flurrying about - the flotilla of ducklings following their mother - the dabchicks or divedappers diving and coming up again.

LORD DENNING   1981

*N*ow for Flies; which is the third bait wherewith Trouts are usually taken. You are to know, that there are so many sorts of flies as there be of fruits: I will name you but some of them; as the dun-fly, the stone-fly, the red-fly, the moor-fly, the tawny-fly, the shell-fly, the cloudy or blackish-fly, the flag-fly, the vine-fly; there be of flies, caterpillars, and canker-flies, and bear-flies; and indeed too many either for me to name, or for you to remember. And their breeding is so various and wonderful, that I might easily amaze mysely, and tire you in a relation of them.

ISAAK WALTON   1653

*L*ast Sunday, we went salmon fishing on the River Test near Southampton, the best salmon pool on the south coast of England. Some of the greatest days of my life have been at Test Wood. I'm not a great believer in flogging the water if the conditions aren't right, so we didn't fish much - there was too much water. Luke was spinning with an artificial lure, and caught a sea trout very quickly. With a spinner you cast it up stream, count it down, wind it back, so you don't need an understanding of the current. I was working a Devon minnow, which you push out alongside the current, slowly letting it swing around, so it's all about feeling the contour of the bottom. It's a slower method; you have to be more skillful. I fish there every Saturday morning, and I know where the stones are.

MARCO PIERRE WHITE   2000

This old hunting ground of Kings has been called "New" since just after the Norman invasion of 1066. With a strange kind of English conceit it will never be called Old Forest. William the Conquerer established his capital in Winchester and the New Forest was near enough to make it a regular hunting place. Not content with the areas of wild land where deer roamed freely the King ordered houses, farms and whole villages to be cleared to increase the area for hunting. Harsh punishments were exacted for breaching any number of special Forest laws. For poaching the King's deer the penalty was death.

What the penalty was for assassination was probably even worse. Whether the shooting of William Rufus was accidental or not Walter Tyrell was taking no chances and fled the country straight away. William's younger brother immediately rode to Winchester and seized power before his older brother could arrive from France. Historians still debate whether the accident was a bit too contrived.

Different laws, rules and regulations created a unique type of social network. In medieval times the number of rights, privileges, rules, laws, regulations, customs and patronage states created a bewildering variety of lifestyles, duties, hopes, ambitions and expectations. Feudalism ruled everyone's lives for a long time after the feudal era had passed elsewhere.

In the early days the forest was managed to provide the best hunting. As such it was not what we would now think of as a managed area of trees. Deer needed open grazing too. The hunters also liked to ride across open country. The forest is mostly flat heathland relieved by a few small streams and rivers. Settlements are scattered without much rhyme or reason except to keep them out of William's way while hunting.

Lyndhurst is the centrally placed administrative hub of the New Forest. It is here that the Verderer's Court sits to decide forest disputes and administer forest laws. In Norman times members of the hunting parties would hang their emblematic shields outside the Inns where they were staying. Flags and banners would also give the town a carnival air.

Here stood the oak tree on which an arrow shot by Sir Walter Tyrrell at a stag glanced and struck King William the Second surnamed Rufus on the breast of which he instantly died on the second day of August anno 1100.

King William the Second surnamed Rufus being slain as before related was laid on a cart, belonging to one Purkis, and drawn from hence, to Winchester, and buried in the Cathedral Church, of that city.

That the spot where an event so memorable might not hereinafter be forgotten the enclosed stone was set up by John Lord Delaware who has seen the tree growing in the place.

JOHN, LORD DELAWARE   1745

So after dinner he took his gun and walked out into the forest, that he might indulge in his reveries. He walked on, quite unconscious of the direction in which he was going, and more than once finding his hat knocked off his head by the branch of a tree which he had not perceived - for the best of all possible reasons, because his eyes were cast on the ground - when his ears were saluted with the neighing of a horse. He looked up, and perceived that he was near to a herd of forest ponies, the first that he had seen since he had lived in the forest.

CAPTAIN MARRYAT   1847

The Children of the New Forest

The Forest has been known and loved by a limited number of persons always; the general public have only discovered it in recent years. For one visitor twenty years ago there are scores, probably hundreds, to-day. And year by year, as motoring becomes more common, and as cycling from being general grows, as it will, to be universal, the flow of visitors to the Forest will go on at an ever-increasing rate, and the hundreds of to-day will be thousands in five years' time. With these modern means of locomotion, there is no more attractive spot than this hundred and fifty square miles of level country which contains the most beautiful forest scenery in England.

W H HUDSON   1923

*H*ampshire hogs are allowed by all for the best bacon. Here the swine feed in the forest on plen-ty of acorns, which, going out lean, return home fat, without care or cost to their owners

FULLER   1661

*G*rintie, grintie, grunt,
Oos be arl tew blunt;
Naw oose Hampshire hogs,
But to zhow the way in bogs.

ANON

◀ *New Forest Foal*

Pig searching for acorns ▶

The path which the young clerk had now to follow lay through a magnificent forest of the very heaviest timber, where the giant boles of oak and of beech formed long aisles in every direction, shooting up their huge branches to build the majestic arches of Nature's own cathedral. Beneath lay a broad carpet of the softest and greenest moss, flecked over with fallen leaves, but yielding pleasantly to the foot of the traveller. The track which guided him was one so seldom used that in places it lost itself entirely among the grass, to reappear as a reddish rut between the distant tree trunks. It was very still here in the heart of the woodlands. The gentle rustle of the branches and the distant cooing of pigeons were the only sounds which broke in upon the silence, save that once Alleyne heard afar off a merry call upon a hunting bugle and the shrill yapping of the hounds.

SIR ARTHUR CONAN DOYLE   1891

The White Company

A nd what is peculiar to the New Forrest and known no where else
are these Brouce Deare; at these severall Lodges the Keepers
gather Brouce and at certaine tymes in the day by a call gathers all
the Dear in within the railes which belongs to each Lodge and so
they come up and feed upon this Brouce and are by that meanes very
fatt and very tame so as to come quite to eate out of your hand; all
the day besides they range about and if they meete any body, if it be
their own keeper, without the pail of the Lodge they will run from
him as wild as can be; these Lodges are about 4 miles asunder and
its a great priviledge and advantage to be a Cheefe Keeper of any of
these Lodges, they have venison as much as they please and can
easily shoote it when the troop comes up with in the paile, for none
are allowed to shoot out in the Forrest nor are allowed to go out
with gun or dog, or to keep any, except Gentlemen, and not they if
they have been found shooteing in the Forrest; I think its Fellony for
any to kill the kings dear; there are severall Rangers of the Forrest;
and 6 Verderers that are their justices or judges of all matters
relateing to the Forrest, these ought allwayes to reside in the Forest
and are to attend the king when he comes into the New Forrest,
clothed in green; they have a Buck and Doe every year for their fee
besides being Masters; the under keepers are at their beck so that
they can get as much venison as they want;...

CELIA FIENNES   1685-1696

◀ *Beehive Cottage, Lyndhurst*
Thatched Cottage ▶

This waſt and wild Part of the Country was, as ſome Record, layʼd open, and waſt for a Foreſt, and for Game, by the violent Tyrant William the Conqueror, and for which purpoſe he un-peopled the Country, pullʼd down the Houſes, and which was worſe, the Churches of ſeveral Pariſhes or Towns, and of abundance of Villages, Turning the poor People out of their Habitations, and Poſſeſſions, and laying all open for his Deer:

DANIEL DEFOE   1727

The photographer at work in Hampshire

PHOTO NOTES

Although most of the photographs in this book date from this year a few were taken on earlier forays into Hampshire. My style often depends on using the first light of dawn to enhance the intensity of colours and textures and cast interesting shadows. I abhor the tendency of photographers in books like this to give paragraphs of technical detail. My most important pieces of equipment are a map, an alarm clock and a compass. Being there is the only advice I can give.

ATMOSPHERE also publish other books
of Bob Croxford's photographs in the
same general format

All the books can be ordered at any
good bookshop.
In case of difficulty phone 01326 240180 or
email books@atmosphere.co.uk

FROM CORNWALL WITH LOVE   *ISBN 09521850 0 8*
FROM DEVON WITH LOVE   *ISBN 09521850 1 6*
FROM BATH WITH LOVE   *ISBN 09521850 2 4*
FROM DORSET WITH LOVE   *ISBN 09521850 3 2*
FROM THE COTSWOLDS WITH LOVE   *ISBN 09521850 4 8*
A VIEW OF AVALON   *ISBN 09521850 6 7*

THE CORNISH COAST (115 x 165 size)   *ISBN 09521850 7 5*

INDEX

The CAPITAL LETTER entries are photographs.

ACKNOWLEDGEMENTS

Many thanks to Karen and Julie for all their help.

The County library in Winchester were helpful during the research for this book. So too were
the many websites devoted to things of Hampshire

Anna Jackson allowed the use of the photograph of Gilbert White's house in Selborne.
The cricket match on Broadhalfpenny Down was photographed by permission of Broadhalfpenny Down Brigands Cricket Club

The quotation from IN PALE BATTALIONS by Robert Goddard published by Bantam Press is reproduced by kind permission of Robert Goddard
The quotation by Emily Loader from PORTSMOUTH VOICES by Robert Cook is reproduced by kind permission of Tempus Publishing Limited
The quotation from ENGLISH FABRIC by F J Harvey Darton originally published by George
Newnes Ltd is reproduced by kind permission of J C Michael Darton
The quotation from WATERSHIP DOWN by Richard Adams published by Penguin is reproduced by kind permission of David Higham Associates
The quotation from THE OLD ROAD by Hilaire Belloc published by Constable is reproduced by kind permission of Peter, Fraser & Dunlop
The quotation from THE FAMILY STORY by Lord Denning published by Butterworths is reproduced by kind permission of
Professor Denning and Peter Post
The quotation from THE KINGDOM BY THE SEA by Paul Theroux is reproduced by kind permission of Penguin UK Ltd
The quotation from ENGLISH JOURNEY by J B Priestley, published by William Heinemann
is reprinted by kind permission of The Random House Group Ltd
The quotation from HAMPSHIRE WITH THE ISLE OF WIGHT, by Arthur Mee. Facsimile edition copyright the
Estate of Arthur Mee and The King's England Press. See www.kingsengland.com
The extract from an interview in Life Support with Marco Pierre White by Stephanie Dennison
(Life, Observer, Sunday 25 June 2000) is reproduced by permission of The Observer
The quotation from IN SEARCH OF ENGLAND by H V Morton is reproduced by permission of Methuen Publishing Limited
The quotation from WHAT HAPPENED TO THE CORBETTS? by Nevil Shute published by William Heinemann is reproduced by permission of
A P Watt Ltd on behalf of the Trustees of the Estate of the late N S Norway
The quotation from THE WHEELS OF CHANCE by H G Wells is reproduced by permission of A P Watt Ltd
on behalf of The Literary Executors of the Estate of H G Wells
The quotation from the foreword by Augustus John to THE FOREST AROUND US by Juliette de Bairadi-Levy
is reproduced courtesy of the artist's estate / Bridgeman Art Library

Every effort has been made to contact all the copyright-holders. Should the publishers have made any mistakes in attribution we will be
pleased to make the necessary arrangements at the first opportunity.